T0368693

FOUNDATION
Check

INSTILLING GODLY HABITS FOR
OPTIMUM SUCCESS IN LIFE

DEBORAH J. KNOWLES

authorHOUSE®

AuthorHouse™
1663 Liberty Drive
Bloomington, IN 47403
www.authorhouse.com
Phone: 833-262-8899

Published by AuthorHouse 12/03/2024

ISBN: 979-8-8230-3873-7 (sc)
ISBN: 979-8-8230-3872-0 (e)

Library of Congress Control Number: 2024925035

Print information available on the last page.

This book is printed on acid-free paper.

Graphic Artist: Geek Digital Creative Agency (242-552-8058)
Editor: Sharita L. Murphy

I dedicate this book to my late father,
Athelston Eric Grazette, AKA Teddy
My wonderful mother, Pearl L. Grazette
My brothers Sean & Wayne Grazette
My beautiful daughter Davinya Shalomi Grazette
and New Converts all over the world!

Follow me on YouTube, Facebook and Instagram.
Purchase my book on Amazon!

Contents

Special thanks ...

Holy Spirit my sweet inspiration

My HDC family! Worship, love and phenomenal teaching anointing dominates Harvest Discipleship Center (HDC), Nassau, Bahamas. To my Lead Pastor Charles Gibson and his wonderful wife Elder Clevette Gibson & my Executive Pastor Jeffrey Rolle and his wonderful wife Deacon Kira Rolle, the ministers and members. God bless the day I found you. Thank you for being the wind beneath my wings. Love you like cooked food, now and always!

To Pastor Dr. Eddie Connor Jr, visionary leader of the Eagles Academy and my Eagles Family. I will always be grateful for your love and support.

Foreword

There comes a time in every believer's journey when we must stop and examine the ground beneath our feet. Are we truly standing on solid ground, or have we unknowingly begun to build on shaky foundations? This is a question every follower of Christ must face. "Foundation Check" by Deborah Knowles is more than just a book; it is a heartfelt, Spirit-led guide to examining the core of our spiritual lives.

As a spiritual leader, I have witnessed firsthand the incredible transformation that takes place when individuals, especially women of faith, align themselves with God's principles and uncover any cracks that may have formed over time. Deborah Knowles, my beloved spiritual daughter, has poured her heart into these pages, with wisdom birthed from her own experiences, triumphs, and challenges. She writes with the authenticity that only comes from a life lived in pursuit of God's truth.

This book will challenge you to pause, reflect, and rebuild where necessary. With each chapter, you will find yourself invited into a deeper relationship with God, as Deborah lovingly guides you through practical steps, biblical insights, and poignant reflections. This journey is not always easy, but it is vital. For just as a strong house must rest upon a firm foundation, so too must our spiritual lives be anchored in Christ.

"Foundation Check" is not just for those who are new in their walk with God; it is for anyone who seeks to strengthen their faith and ensure that their life is firmly rooted in the Word. Whether you are just starting your journey or have been walking with the Lord for years, this book is a gift—a spiritual tool that will help you assess, repair, and fortify the foundation upon which your faith stands.

I am immensely proud of Deborah Knowles and the work God is doing through her. As you read these pages, may you be inspired to dig deep, strengthen your spiritual foundation, and allow God to do a new work in your life.

With love and blessings,
Sherilyn Fletcher
Spiritual Mother

We are living in times where life is fickle and fragile, now more than ever before. The saying used to be "Here today, gone tomorrow." Now it's here today, gone today. The phraseology extends beyond how long one lives, to furthermore how well one lives.

Scripture affirms, "Beloved, I wish above all things that thou mayest prosper and be in health, even as thy soul prospereth" (3 John 1:2). We cannot truly prosper emotionally, mentally, physically, financially, and relationally if we are out of position spiritually, lacking our foundation in Christ.

Undoubtedly, your fruit of lack thereof is indicative of your foundation. This book provides the necessary spiritual tools to win the battle against your mind and future. Building a fruitful future begins by developing a solid foundation.

Deborah Knowles knows the power of a Foundation Check to enlighten the eyes of our understanding through the Word of God. The name Deborah is renowned as a significant figure in scripture. Deborah was the only female to serve as a prophet and judge for her people.

God has raised up a new generation Deborah to declare the Word of the Lord, locally and globally. She is anointed to unashamedly and unabashedly shift you from obscurity into opportunity.

As you reach deep into the resourcefulness of this book, you will discover that every page is personalized. In every chapter, I expect your mind to be renewed, your heart to be restored, your prayer life to be revived, and repentance to rejuvenate your spirit.

God has equipped Deborah with an impactful word to transform your world. Apply the spiritual strategies of Foundation Check and remain in divine alignment with your God-given assignment, so you can win from within.

Foreword by Dr. Eddie Connor Jr

Introduction

Foundation Check is about taking an introspective look at the foundation of your life and making the necessary changes to support success. Success in this context is living at your full potential. In the construction of a building, the foundation is paramount to the building's ability to withstand storms and natural disasters of all kinds. This book attempts to bring a greater awareness of the importance of a strong foundation in prayer, fasting, praise and worship, meditation, and personal Bible study. These activities are important if you want to have a victorious life. This book requires that you be accountable. This book speaks to the person in the mirror.

We can all agree that we can see a sun in the sky during the day and a moon in the sky during night. So let us build on our place of agreement to acknowledge that there must be an all-knowing, all-powerful, all-loving heavenly Father who is watching *you*! And He is calling *you* into a place of *accountability*!

Are you willing to die for the gospel of Jesus Christ of Nazareth? Because it will take death to the dictates of your flesh! This will ensure that the foundation of your life pleases your Creator! Don't fear the one who can kill the flesh; rather, fear He who can destroy both body and soul.

If your answer is *yes*, here is your action plan: prayer, fasting, praise and worship, personal Bible study, and meditation. These actions are foundational requirements, and *Foundation Check* will keep you on course to developing a strong foundation in Christ Jesus!

The weapons of our warfare are not carnal; rather, they are mighty through God for the pulling down of strongholds. Prayer, a combination of prayer and fasting, a combination of praise and worship, Bible study, and meditation are spiritual weapons. The objective is to be a skillful soldier in the army of the Lord. Possess your possession and defeat the enemy on every turn. *Foundation Check* will help you *win*!

One of the tactics of the enemy is to force you to self-destruct! This happens through identity crisis. In order to counterattack the plans of the enemy you have to use the gates to your mind (they are the eye, mouth, ears, and skin) for righteousness and not evil. When with your eye gate, you read and study the Word of God, you will find information that you need to succeed. This is how Foundation Check works.

John 1:12 -13 KJV says "But as many as received him, to them gave he power to become the sons of God, even to them that believe on his name: Which were born, not of blood, nor of the will of the flesh, nor of the will of man, but of God." This says you are a child of God. So engage your reasoning abilities and you will find that as a child of God, you have rights as a believer. Then you can open your mouth in prayer, declarations, and affirmations and create the world that is rightly and fully yours using the word of God that you have read, studied, and meditated upon.

Out of the abundance of the heart (imagination, thoughts, reasoning, intellect, and memories), the mouth speaks. This is not any ordinary speaking; it is the same speaking that God did as recorded in Genesis 1:15 KJV "And let them be for lights in the firmament of the heaven to give light upon the earth: and it was so." This passage describes God's creation of the sun, moon and stars.

The word *abundance* describes a lifestyle. This is not a hit-and-miss sort of thing that comes once a year or an SOS to be used only in times of emergency. This is a "give us this day our *daily* bread" situation (Matthew 6:11 KJV)—a daily walk with the Lord. It's called a *lifestyle*! And that's how *Foundation Check* works. So, if you are up for the challenge, let's do this! We can do all things by the *power* of Almighty God!

PART 1
Soil Check! √

The objective of this section is to prepare the soil of your heart with several truths and revelations to embrace change. The Bible asks if we can know the truth without a teacher or preacher. Philip asked the eunuch if he understood what he was reading. The eunuch then asked for Philip's guidance (see Acts 8:30–31 KJV).

You need to understand why *Foundation Check* is important and how it fits into the big scheme of things. What is your role, and what it's going to take for you to succeed?

CHAPTER 1

The Big Picture

God wants a family! God is love. He does not *have* love; He *is* love. The agape love of God is unconditional. There is nothing you can do to change it. With agape love, your best interest is at the center of all God does and allows. In other words, He ensures that whatever comes your way, you have the ability and capacity to win! He prepares you for what's ahead and sets you up to be better than you were when you approach any given challenge. His love for us is invincible and amazing!

True love must have a recipient. That is where you and I come in. As a matter of fact, God's entire creation demonstrates His glory, splendor, and majesty. Father God takes care of all His creation from the ant to the rhinoceros and from the sea to the sky. The universe is His handiwork, and it's all because of His love for us. Humankind is the pride of His creation because He made us in His image and likeness. Then He gave us dominion. This dominion is authority to rule and manage all creation. As you can see, we are doing just that, which is our God-given right.

There was a war in heaven between Father God and Lucifer, who convinced a third of the angel population to follow him, and Lucifer (Satan) and his crew were thrown out of heaven. The war was so great the earth was devastated, but God recreated, as told in the book of Genesis. "In the beginning God created the heavens and the earth. Now the earth was formless and empty, darkness was over the surface of the deep, and the Spirit of God was hovering over the waters." (Genesis 1:1-2 NIV). This means the earth was chaotic, devastated and filled with darkness. But there was hope because the Spirit of God moved upon the face of the dark waters and God said ...

I must pause right here to point out to you that, when you experience chaos and devastation in your life, it's not time for a pity party! It is an opportunity to use the creative powers God gave you. This is evident when He said, "Let us make man in our image, after our likeness" (Genesis 1:26 KJV).

God crowned the week of creation with His greatest creation: humankind. He gave humankind a *purpose*: to be fruitful, multiply, and replenish the earth, subdue it, and have dominion over the fish of the sea and the birds of the air. His purpose has not changed. It is still relevant today.

Humankind's archenemy will forever be Satan because the Owner/Creator Father God gave us dominion and power on the earth when He was here first. Satan feels slighted, so to speak. Therefore, he hates us and will always hate us with a cruel hatred that can never be quenched. Satan set up a parallel kingdom to God's, and his objectives are to kill, steal from, and destroy humankind. Satan seems to be doing a pretty good job. If we keep track of world news and events, we will find overwhelming evidence of this.

Deborah J. Knowles

This chart illustrates satan's opposing tactics:

God (original Creator)	satan (pervert truth)
Creator	perversion
Good	evil
Humility	pride
Heaven	hell
All-powerful	powerless (unless you empower)
Abundance	lack/poverty
Love	hatred
Truth	lies
Pure	deceitful

CHAPTER 2
The Holy Ghost's Role

God promised that, if we acknowledge Him in all our ways, He will direct our paths. Acknowledgment is the beginning of real change. You must come to the realization that there are issues in your foundation. Confront them. Don't ignore them. They are there for a reason: to kill, to steal, and to destroy. Sooner or later, they will do just that.

What does acknowledgment look like? Here is an example: "Lord, I have an issue with lying, cussing, smoking, and lust. Please help me to overcome these fleshly tendencies by Your power. I acknowledge the exchange that happened on the cross when my Lord and Savior died so that I don't have to live in sin. Father, manifest Your deliverance from evil in my life. I will do whatever it takes for as long as it takes." This is what acknowledgment looks like!

Holy Spirit is your personal Guide and Helper. He leads you into all truth—truth about yourself, your bondage and chains, your bloodline, and your destiny. He knows the weaknesses and strengths that have been passed down to you through your lineage, and He wants to help you. Once you make Him feel at home, He will stick with you through thick and thin. He will help you make wise choices, when you must make decisions about a life partner, your finances, your ministry, your health, and all other important issues in your life. He is your personal counselor, and He promises never to leave you or forsake you.

Holy Spirit possesses miracle-working power, and He has kings' hearts in His hand. He is the administrator of all the desires of Father God concerning you. He knows your case quite well. The plans of Father God are His plans as well. He and Father God are of one mind and one agenda; there is no division among Them.

Holy Spirit is trustworthy and dependable. He will not let you down. In His time, He makes all things beautiful. He is a friend who sticks closer than a brother. All He requires is that you put Him first. Make Him a priority in your life. He wants to be your best friend.

To maximize your relationship with Holy Spirit, you must practice trusting Him and *not* leaning on your own understanding. He moves in ways that are unprecedented. Just let Him have His way! *Trust* Him!

CHAPTER 3

The Growth Process

Patience, persistence, and forgiving yourself are the key elements that secure your spiritual growth on your part, and the Holy Spirit will take care of the rest.

A wise man once said, "Patience is when you're supposed to get mad, but you choose to understand instead." Not only must you be patient with others, but you must also be patient with yourself. The Merriam-Webster dictionary defines *patient* as "bearing pains or trails calmly or without complaint." A patient person is steadfast despite opposition, difficulty, and adversity. A patient person is able or willing to bear adversity. The battle zone that you have entered is won with patience. Patience is one of your greatest weapons, and you must learn early in your walk with God how to use it. "Consider it pure joy, my brothers and sisters, whenever you face trials of many kinds, because you know that the testing of your faith produces perseverance." James 1:2-3 NIV

According to this scripture, if you allow patience to have its way, you will lack nothing.

Prayer point: "Father, let patience have its perfect way in me."

Another ingredient in your growth process is persistence. Persistence exists continually or for a longer-than-usual period of time. There is a story in the Bible of a widow and an unjust judge. She was persistent in her request from this judge, and she followed up many times until he gave her what she wanted. This story teaches us to be persistent in prayer. Your persistence, diligence, and focus show God that your request is what you really desire. At difficult times in life, you may want to give up and throw in the towel. That's the time to push harder and longer. This is persistence.

Another ingredient is faith. "Now faith is the substance of things hoped for, the evidence of things not seen." Heb. 11:1 KJV. It is impossible to please God without faith. Faith is evident in your life as works because faith with no works is dead faith. "And without faith it is impossible to please God, because anyone who comes to him must believe that he exists and that he rewards those who earnestly seek him." Hebrews 11:6 NIV. *Foundation Check* will assist you in developing your faith.

Prayer point: "Father, I believe. Help my unbelief."

In the growth process, we must be diligent. Diligence is the antidote for laziness, slothfulness, and procrastination. These types of behavior will land you in hell. Matthew 25:26 tells the parable of the talents. Jesus said, "His lord answered and said unto him, Thou wicked and slothful servant, thou knewest that I reap where I sowed not, and gather where I have not strawed:" Verse 30 continues, "And cast that unprofitable servant into outer darkness: there shall be weeping and gnashing of teeth." KJV That's called hell. Merriam-Webster defines *diligence* as "steady, earnest, and energetic effort." Diligent people often work toward a goal (a SMARTER goal). They do not allow life to just pass by while they wait for good things to fall into their laps without any effort of their own.

Prayer point: "Father, make my hands diligent."

PART 2
Quality Check! √

God's purpose has not changed toward humankind. He desires to dwell among His people and commune with them friend to friend according to Exodus 25:8.

The season of grace is soon to come to an end. Seek the Lord while He may be found. Call upon Him while He is near. This is an urgent call, a clarion call, a call you need to make a priority.

There is a saying in computer science that goes, "Garbage in, garbage out." In a natural foundation, the cement mix is critical to the quality of the foundation you build. For example, on an island, builders who seek to cut costs will get sand from the beach to mix into the cement they will use for the foundation. After a while, the salt in the sand will erode the foundation. But a good foundation can sustain the structure placed upon it.

As it is naturally, so it is spiritually. You must build a lifestyle of prayer, fasting, praise, worship, meditation, and personal Bible study into your spiritual foundation that will sustain the purpose of God for your life.

"The Wise Man and the Foolish Man" is a hymn written by Ann Omley in 1948. Here are some of the lyrics:

The wise man built his house upon the Rock,
The wise man built his house upon the Rock,
The wise man built his house upon the Rock,
And the rains came tumbling down.
The rains came down and the floods came up,
The rains came down and the floods came up,
The rains came down and the floods came up,
But the house on the Rock stood firm.

Remember that Father God is always trying to get something to us. We are in a deficit. We are the ones that *fell* from glory, and He has done all He can to restore us! But He needs your cooperation, your agreement, your body, your life! Will you let Him use you to restore all that was stolen from you?

One of the benefits of a firm foundation in Christ is that we can remain standing after the storm passes over—after the bad doctor's report, financial troubles, marriage problems, church hurt, mind battles, etc. Jesus told His flock to be of good cheer because He had overcome the world (John 16:33). We are more than conquerors because of Jesus Christ's finished work on the cross.

The benefits of these principles enter your life only through doing or application. I always like to use the analogy of a box of hair color for the ladies and maybe some shaving cream for the men. Nothing happens until the product comes out of the box and you become intimate with it; in other words, it touches or interacts with you. The product has the ingredients to produce the results you are looking for. The hair color will brighten, and the shaving cream will smooth the removal of unwanted hair, but if liken to this metaphor there is no application, there will be no revelation, or change in your life. Application is the key to change!

Get a mirror and look at yourself eyeball to eyeball and tell yourself, "I am getting ready to change!" We will apply the Word of God to our thought life, and there will be a chemical reaction. Transformation will follow mind renewal. It's guaranteed. Get excited and put a praise on it!

These Godly habits will create portals in your life for an exchange to happen. A portal is a doorway, a gate, a place of transfer. An example in the Bible is found in Genesis 28:12. Jacob dreamed about a ladder set up on the earth. It reached to heaven, and the angels of God used it to ascend and descend. Wow this is a gateway! Another gateway was the Virgin Mary being impregnated with baby Jesus! Heaven is always reaching out to us to bless us and keep us safe! But you *must* decide to enter that realm. It's a members-only club based on your choices. Your actions will always speak louder than your words. Make a decision to become a member of the family of God.

When you make that decision, you are acknowledging and praising Jesus for dying on the cross. You are cashing in your check so to speak. When you accept Jesus Christ as your Lord and Savior, you receive a blank check, a promissory note. You apply your faith by cashing it in, making good on the promises of God.

The veil in the temple was rent from top to bottom sending the message that Father God has taken care of everything that would come between Him and us because He wants to be our friend. He has done his part; He wants to know if we feel the same way about Him. Father God has taken care of everything that can ever hinder our relationship with Him. We just must believe it by living through *faith* in His Word. Faith without work is dead. So, let's get to work!

Action	Benefit
Personal praise and worship	God lives. The greatest power on earth dwells in you
Personal prayer	Information and power
Personal prayer and fasting	Faster manifestation of God's will
Personal Bible study	Enlightenment understanding
Personal meditation	Transformation
Fellowship with the saints	Iron sharpens iron

Precious child of God's creation, God does not want to be distant from you! He has gone to great lengths to deal with what stands between you and Him. Please come close, draw near to God, and He will draw near to you. He asked me to insert the word *personal* in this chart to let you know that He is your personal Savior. To continue that relationship, He needs personal time with you. Corporate worship cannot replace it. There are things He wants to discuss with you that are just between you and Him. It's call intimacy! "Come closer," says the Lord. "You will never be the same again! I promise."

CHAPTER 4

Prayer

The first check in your foundation is prayer. Prayer is simply having a conversation with God. God is the Creator of heaven and earth and the universe, and He seeks a relationship with you.

That's a wow moment! We get excited when the Queen comes to town, or we visit government house or get to meet our favorite celebrity. Why? Because it gives us a sense of importance or prosperity. But we seem to think very little of meeting with the Almighty God, King of kings and Lord of lords, the Owner of the Universe! This is a big deal! You can't get any more important than that, and here is the clincher: He wants to meet with you! He makes time for you! As a matter of fact, he made planet Earth for you to live on and enjoy. All He asks for in return is that you acknowledge Him always and He will direct your path.

Don't you think His 'resume' indicates that He is the most qualified Person to direct your path? I think it does, in a great way! In a nutshell, He created you and the planet. Now He wants to show you how to enjoy it to the fullest! Wow! What a mighty good God!

How does prayer work? Prayer is a portal or gateway through which transfers happen. For example, David prayed and asked God to create in him a clean heart. He asked God to renew in him a right spirit. David was asking Almighty God to take his lying, deceiving, murdering heart—his actions and thoughts—and give him clean, pure love with which he could seek the best interest of others.

As you develop your prayer life, there will be a transfer of power that will save you from sin and give you a more Godlike character. Stealing will change to giving, lying will change to speaking the truth. As your relationship with God develops, just as it does in any other relationship, trust will develop. You will begin to do more for God. You will begin to walk in greater obedience. You will experience greater levels of faith in God. Prayer gives you power to change.

Matthew 6:5 -13 gives us the template for prayer. A template is a form or guide, or pattern we use to make something. Before we review the template, the scripture tells us that the most powerful place to pray is in your closet, which just means a private, quiet place. What is done secretly is rewarded openly. Another key to prayer that gets results is not to include any vain babbling, which is useless words or ramblings. Get straight to the point. Prayer points are highly recommended; you can search online for prayer points on any topic you need. God continues to say that He knows what you need better than you do. He just wants acknowledgement in prayer. Your prayers to Him show Him that you need His help and that you acknowledge Him as your Source and your Creator.

The template reads like this: "Our Father which is in heaven, Hallowed be thy name. Thy kingdom come, Thy will be done on earth, as it is in heaven. Give us this day our daily bread. And forgive us our debts, as we forgive our debtors. And lead us not to temptation but deliver us from evil: For thine is the kingdom, and the power, and the glory, forever. Amen." Matthew 6:5-13 KJV

The key to using a template is that you must fill in the blanks with your own words in accordance with the situation you are currently going through when you pray. For example, if you received a diagnosis of diabetes at your annual checkup, you could follow these three steps:

Step 1: Go into your prayer closet because you want a public demonstration of God's power.

Step 2: Show God the doctor's report and ask Holy Spirit to guide you according to the Word of God to pray. Perhaps Holy Spirit would lead you to the story of the woman who had suffered with the issue of blood for twelve long years. This story is found in Mark 5:25 – 29 KJV. After reading this story numerous times and studying the scripture, you will learn that the hem of Jesus's robe, which she touched, represents the Ten Commandments. Then meditate on the scripture.

Step 3: Your prayer would go something like this:

Our Father which art in heaven.

You created me and You are not confined to the dictates of this world.

Hallowed be thy name.

Father, there is nothing too hard for you. You are the God who took nothing and made something. You are awesome in all Your ways. All creation shows Your splendor.

Thy kingdom come, Thy will be done on earth, as it is in heaven.

Father, there is no sickness in heaven where You are; there is only fullness of joy. I want Your kingdom to reign in my life on earth. Heal me of this diabetes.

Give us this day our daily bread.

Show me what to do and what to say to be rid of this disease.

And forgive us our debts, as we forgive our debtors.

Father, please forgive my sins against You and humankind. I release all who offended me.

And lead us not into temptation but deliver us from evil.

Father do not let my faith waver. Do not let me resort to a compromise for my healing; rather, let me be steadfast in prayer and fasting and wait on You. I will not spend all the money I have on doctor bills. Please deliver me from evil.

For thine is the kingdom, and the power, and glory forever. Amen

Father, I trust You. Amen

As a disciple of Jesus Christ, you have a responsibility to do greater works. John 14:12 says "Truly, truly, I say to you, whoever believes in me will also do the works that I do; and greater works than these will he do, because I am going to the Father" (ESV).

How do we perform these works with power, and where do we get this power in prayer? A disciple of Jesus Christ is a follower of Jesus Christ. Followers have developed lifestyles of prayer, fasting, meditation, and study of God's Word.

We need God's power demonstrated on earth to defeat the enemy, but first we must submit to the will and way of power. James 4:7 KJV says, "Submit therefore to God. Resist the devil, and he will flee from you." Without submission there will be no fleeing!

If the devil is not moving, ask the Holy Spirit to reveal to you the areas in which you have not submitted. Do a foundation check! You will not be able to complete our assignment in this life without the power of God. We have an enemy that opposes everything that is of God. He hides in ignorance and disobedience. Why does he hide? Because God is the greatest power, and the Bible declares that Father God will not allow us to be ignorant of the devices of the enemy.

A lifestyle of prayer will make you a victor and not a victim! Prayer is not hindered by distance, time, or space. Prayer is an incredible, dynamic power of God at work in humankind. Take hold of this mighty weapon and watch lives change and transform for the glory of God!

Here is an action plan to jump start your prayer life!

5:30 am: Set your alarm and get up and pray. Refer to Psalm 63:1- 8

6:00 am: Open your Bible and read, then study scripture.

6:30 am: Start getting ready for work.

Send feedback to foundation√@gmail.com. I want to hear from you especially about the areas that are the most challenging.

There are many types of prayers including thanksgiving, affirmations, declarations, warfare, petition, and praise. I have provided a summary chart below: -

Thanksgiving	Giving God thanks
Affirmations	Confessing the Bible
Declaration	Agreeing with the Bible
Warfare	Deliverance from evil
Petition	Asking God for something
Praise	Adoring and magnifying God

CHAPTER 5

Fasting and Prayer

In Matthew 17:21, we read "But this kind of demon won't leave unless you have prayed and gone without food" (TLB). There was a father who had a son who suffered with mental health condition. He would throw himself into the fire and into the water. He was violent and always angry. The father took his son to Jesus' disciples and asked them to deliver his son from the demon that was affecting his son, but the disciples were unable to help him. Then the father went to Jesus and told Him of all that had happen, and Jesus asked the man to bring the child to Him. Jesus rebuked the demon, and the demon left the boy that very instant. The boy was healed. The disciples then asked Jesus why they had not been able to cure the boy, and He responded that a demon such as the one that had controlled the boy could be driven out only through prayer and fasting.

Prayer and fasting represent another level of submission to God. The combination brings the flesh under submission. Food provides energy for the flesh to function, but when we pray and fast, we tap into the operation of the power or energy of Holy Ghost. We are saying to the flesh that there is no need for natural power; instead, we want supernatural power. As believers, we tap into miracles, signs, and wonders!

Fasting and prayer are a powerful combination. You cannot have an effective fast without prayer. When we fast, we set aside food to feed our spiritual bodies and starve our physical bodies. We do this to pull from the storehouse of heaven whatever we need.

Jesus was asked why the disciples of John, and the Pharisees fasted, but His disciples did not. Jesus answered that His disciples need not fast while the bridegroom (Himself) was with them. When He was absent from them, they could fast (Mark 2:18-20). In other words, neither John nor the Pharisees were considered the bridegroom. Jesus was the Bridegroom, the church was His bride, and He would return for the marriage feast. In addition, we must understand that, when we fast, it is always for the Kingdom of God to reign on earth.

God's purpose for fasting is found in Isaiah 58 especially verses 6 and 7.

To lose the bands of wickedness

To undo heavy burdens

To let the oppressed go free

To break every yoke

To deal thy bread to the hunger

To bring the cast out poor to your house

To clothe the naked

To hide not thyself from thy own flesh

God's response:

Thy light break forth

Thy health spring forth speedily

Thy righteousness go before thee

The glory of the Lord thy rear guard

The Lord will guide thee continually

Satisfy thy soul in drought

Make thy bones fat ...

There are types of fasts that are biblically based that you can use based on their context.

The Disciple's Fast loses the bands of wickedness. (Matthew 17:21).

Ezra Fast relieves heavy burdens. (Ezra 8:23).

The Samuel Fast lets the oppressed go free. (1 Samuel 7:6).

Elijah Fast breaks every yoke. (1 Kings 19:4–8).

Widow's Fast shares bread with the hungry. (1 Kings 17:16).

Saint Paul Fast allows God's light to break forth like the morning. (Acts 9:9).

Daniel Fast encourages your health to spring. (Daniel 1:8).

John the Baptist fast ensures that your righteousness goes before. (Luke 1:15).

Esther Fast ensures that the glory of the Lord shall protect us. (Esther 4:16; 5:2).

Please study and use these portals of power where they are needed in your journey with the Lord to bring His Name glory!

When we set aside a period to fast, we set aside time to feed our spiritual bodies for a specified purpose, which advances the Kingdom of God in our lives or in the lives of others.

Humans are spirits who live in bodies and possess souls. Our Creator declares "Let us make man [mankind] in our image and after our likeness" (Genesis 1:26 KJV). Father God is a God of spirits; therefore, He can influence every heart.

Fasting enables us to operate in our true selves and bring to the forefront the purpose and plan of God for our lives and the lives of others. When we walk after the Spirit, we will not fulfill the lust of the flesh. The Spirit brings life, but the flesh brings death and decay.

Fasting God's way loosens the bands of wickedness, lessens heavy burdens, frees the oppressed, and breaks yokes. Refer to Isaiah 58.

Prayer and fasting are inseparable. When we fast, we humble ourselves and pray in obedience to the Word of God. As we read in 2 Chronicles 7:14, when we turn from our wicked ways and seek the face of God, He will hear us from His place in heaven and heal our land. This is God's promise.

When we pray and fast, we must declare and decree the promises of God in our lives and in the lives of others. We must earnestly desire that God's Kingdom come and God's will be done. We are walking in Kingdom authority and dominion power that was given to us by Father God. We must accept these gifts. We must take ownership of them and use them to bring honor and glory to God. Our lifestyles must bring honor and glory to God.

Unless the Lord builds the house, we labor in vain. Unless God watches the city, the watchman watches in vain. We must allow God to interfere in our lives and in the lives of others through prayer and fasting to experience true success and productivity in our lives. We must allow the author and finisher of our faith to be Lord of our lives. We do this when we humble ourselves, put aside our agendas, our opinions, and our feelings and let God's way and will reign supreme in our lives. This is how we get the victory in every trial, test, and obstacle in our lives. We must let God be God!

Prayer and fasting enable the power of Almighty God to manifest in your life and in the lives of others. Prayer and fasting are the breeding grounds for miracles, signs, and wonders. Together, they demonstrate the love and goodness of Almighty God.

Prayer and fasting enable revelation to flow, that transform lives. For ministers of the gospel, prayer and fasting should be a lifestyle for this very same reason. As I have mentioned, prayer and fasting bring to the forefront of your life your true self, which reflects the purpose and plans of Almighty God!

Prayer and fasting make you more like Christ. You are most effective in ministry by bringing the flesh under submission of the will of Almighty God for your life.

Live a life of prayer and fasting as the Holy Spirit leads!

CHAPTER 6

Personal Bible Study

In all you're getting, get understanding. When you do not understand the purpose of a thing, you will abuse it, and it will not serve you. You will not receive the blessing that it was programmed to give you.

Personal Bible study fuels your prayer life, and your prayer life reveals and sustains your purpose and assignment.

Every profession is sustained through a time of formal education. In Ephesians 1:18 NIV, we read, "I pray that the eyes of your heart may be enlightened in order that you may know the hope to which he has called you, the riches of his glorious inheritance in his holy people."

While carrying out your assignment, you will encounter attacks; therefore, you must know the weapons of our warfare. I believe personal Bible study is one of them. Because you are armed with knowledge to counterattack, you will be able to thwart the tactics of the enemy.

Personal Bible study is private it is between you and God. It is also personal because you will be dealing with the issues that you experience in your assignment and in your character.

Personal Bible study pulls down the strongholds in your mind. This is the weapon that is mighty through God for the pulling down of strongholds. A stronghold is a negative mental thought pattern. To enlighten our dark understanding, we must give our hearts to the Lord. This includes a commitment to read and study the Bible daily. The Bible is inspired by God; it expresses His thoughts and His ways.

In Isaiah 1:18 KJV we read, "Come now, and let us reason together, saith the Lord: though your sins be as scarlet, they shall be as white as snow; though they be red like crimson, they shall be as wool." The words *let us reason together* means "let us debate our case in court." *Reasoning* refers to your grounds for argument.

2 Timothy 2:15 KJV says, "Study to shew thyself approved unto God, a workman that needed not to be ashamed, rightly dividing the word of truth." Study refers to the setting of the mind or thoughts on a subject.

These two scriptures prove that humankind

was created with the ability to reason and come to conclusions and decisions. This is why Bible study is so important. Our enemy hides in our ignorance and sends smoke screens of shame and condemnation because we do not know. Our not knowing keeps us in a trap. But the Bible declares that, if we reject knowledge, God will reject us. If we choose to reject knowledge, we are choosing to reject God.

Studying the Word of God fills you with enlightenment, peace, and joy. Studying the Word of God teaches you how to win at life by overcoming it's many challenges. Studying the Word of God arms you when you pray that you have a rich supply of the Word in your heart, and you can put God in remembrance of His Word.

When we speak the Word of God on a situation, it will not return to Him void of success; rather, it shall accomplish what it was sent forth to do. It is a win, win situation!

We were shaped in iniquity and in sin did our mothers conceive us (Psalm 51:5 KJV). We sin -miss the goals of the life God ordained for us -naturally and easily. It takes no effort to lie, steal, fornicate, get drunk, etc. That is our nature. It is referred to as the Adamic nature meaning fleshy or earthy. It means that we live to satisfy whatever the flesh wants. The word *Christian* means Christ-like. Therefore, for those of us with a sinful nature to transform to Christ-like persons, we must renew our minds. Renewing the mind means thinking like Christ. This is why He preserved His thoughts in the form of the Bible so that we can think like our Creator and friend. There is no substitute!

The Bible is a collection of history, laws, poetries, prophecies, and letters that encourages and teaches us what to do to obtain optimum success in life. Most importantly, it chronicles the life of Jesus Christ of Nazareth. Jesus shows us how we can enter the Kingdom of God.

Your flesh is a constant enemy of God, and anything associated with God. The devil is your lifelong adversary. The devil can never and will never be your friend, but you can rest assured that God is your friend forever! Your flesh and the adversary will do all they can to stop you from praying, fasting, and most importantly reading God's Word. They will try to make you sleepy and busy, but you must persevere.

Personal Bible study should be separate from group Bible study. Study groups are very motivating and dynamic, but God desires time alone with you! There are many things He wants to teach and show you as an individual so that you can begin doing the will of the Father and complete your assignment. In Matthew 7:21 KJV, we read, "Not everyone that saith unto me, Lord, shall enter in the Kingdom of heaven;

but he that doeth the will of the Father which is in heaven."

Knowing what you were placed on earth to do and getting busy with it will shut out idleness, which opens access to demonic activity. Keeping busy with your assignment will keep you rooted and grounded in God.

There are multiple forms of group Bible study. You might join a group at your church or participate through an online forum. But the foundation of a victorious Christian life is to have personal, one-on-one, quality time with the Lord.

Jesus left His disciples on many occasions and prayed to the Father alone. Jesus is God, and He is our example. He is a God of integrity and does not ask us to do anything He Himself has not done.

Seek the Lord while He may be found and call upon Him while He is near. We can never exhaust the knowledge of God and His dimensions of revelation. God's will is His Word, and we must understand it to apply it to our lives. The Bible encourages us to pray with the understanding so that we do not miss the mark. The Word of God is the sword of the Spirit that we use to combat the plans of the enemy. How can we fight effectively if we do not understand how to use our swords?

Personal Bible study helps us to put on the whole armor of the Lord so that we can stand against the wiles of the enemy and be victorious. For example, in Psalm 119:105, we read, "Thy word is lamp unto my feet and a light unto my path." (KJV) This world is a dark place, and we need a guide so that we do not fall from grace. The Word of God illuminates the path that we should take. A lamp provides just enough light so you can see in front of you. Why? Because this daily walk with the Lord is a walk of faith (blessed assurance). A light gives you direction in your current situation. It illuminates the path that the Lord would have you take. So, there is a light for our steps (feet) and a light for our path (the stance He would like you to take in a particular situation).

Illumination answers these questions: -

Who am I?

Prayer and Bible study go hand in hand. When you ask the Lord who you are, He reveals it in His Word. Knowing who you are in God is knowing your purpose, the very essence of your existence and the assignment you must complete before leaving earth. This is the most fulfilling revelation you could ever receive from the Lord! Knowing who you are and what you were born to do prevent jealousy from raising its ugly head in your life. Slothfulness and procrastination are destroyed because you realize that the King's work requires haste, and each day of your life takes on new meaning and fulfillment. Time wasters and distractions are removed from your life as you walk in purpose. Your spiritual power awakens, and gifts begin to stir as you walk in faith to do the will of the Lord. Your amour comes alive! You are no longer the living dead but have awakened to purpose! Glory to God!

Where am I in Your plan for my life?

God has a spiritual calendar. He is God. He is Creator of heaven and earth. We fit into His plan; He does not fit into ours. Proverbs 19:21NIV tells us, "Many are the plans in a person's heart, but it is the Lord's purpose that prevails." We need to yield to the plans of God for our life. Why? "It is He that hath made us, and not we ourselves" (Psalm 100:3 KJV). He is all knowing. He is all powerful. He is the only One who has enough power and knowledge to make it happen.

And so, because of our disobedience and rebellion we have lost some time, but our prayer should be for the Lord to help us make the most of every opportunity (Ephesians 5:15). We need to make the most of the time we have in this world by making wise decisions according to the council of God's Word. Know and understand that each assignment is for an allotted time. God took us out of eternity and placed us in time so that we may complete assignments that will always include bringing sons to glory to spend eternity with Him! We must work while it is day, because no one can work in the night. We must stay on our watch so

41

that we will hear these words from the Master: Well, done! You can come into your inheritance of eternal life with Me.

Knowing where you are in God's plan now and where you need to be helps you and God to strategize against the delaying tactics of the enemy. In the gates, the enemy is making plans to destroy, delay, and demolish all that God has for you. But you must walk closely with the Lord and keep the channels open, allowing His Word to guide you to victory.

When your life is filled with integrity, you influence others. When your life is filled with praise and adoration to the One true God, you will influence others. It is not God's desire that any should perish, but that all might have everlasting life. This is why He sent His Son, and this is why He is sending you. He will keep sending so that whosoever believes in the Lord Jesus Christ shall not perish. What a wonderful Savior! Are you available to the Lord? Are you available to be His hands extended, to think His thoughts, to be a light and to be the salt? Are you available to be used by God?

Let us submit to His plan right now. Enough time has been lost.

How do I get where I need to be?

Personal Bible study addresses personal issues in your life. It cleanses and prepares you for spiritual success. It helps you to keep a guard over your heart by looking into the mirror of God's Word daily, firstly identifying the areas that are out of alignment and secondly changing so that God will be glorifying in your personal life.

Personal Bible study breaks ungodly cycles in your life by renewing your mind in the Word of God. In Romans 12:2 KJV we read, "And be not conformed to this world: but be ye transformed by the renewing of your mind, that ye may prove what is that good, and acceptable, and perfect, will of God."

Annually we license our vehicles and renew our driver's licenses. It is a way for the government to generate funds to defer cost of managing the roads, traffic lights, etc.

There is an expiry date after which, if we drive our vehicles on government roads, the police may levy a fine upon us.

So it is in the Spirit. Your old way of thinking cannot take you or sustain you in the next dimension and level that the Lord has for you to experience. The devil will destroy you, pick you off, if you lag. Prayer and Bible study will keep you sharp as a tack in the spiritual fight for your soul, and you will be able to evade the plans of the enemy and walk in victory, not only for yourself but for those you influence as well. If you are a believer, you will be victorious! Believing and victory go hand in hand! Do you believe today?

CHAPTER 7

Meditation

When we meditate, we focus our minds so we can think and consider deeply.

Joshua 1:8 KJV "This book of the law shall not depart out of thy mouth; but thou shalt meditate therein day and night, that thou mayest observe to do according to all that is written therein: for then thou shalt make thy way prosperous, and then thou shalt have good success."

The Hebrew word for meditate is *sina*, which means to muse or rehearse in one's mind. Another word that defines meditation is *ruminate*, which means to go over in your mind repeatedly and slowly—to chew again what has been chewed slightly, to chew repeatedly, to chew the cud.

Let us learn from the cow. The website Moo-natomy: The Biology of a Cow (https://www2.

kenyon.edu/projects/farmschool/food/milkbio.htm)
explains the digestive system of a cow.

> The cow has four stomachs and
> undergoes a special digestive process
> to break down the tough and coarse
> food it eats. When the cow first eats, it
> chews the food just enough to swallow
> it. The unchewed food travels to the
> first two stomachs, the rumen, and
> the reticulum, where it is stored until
> later. When the cow is full of this eating
> process, she rests. Later, the cow
> coughs up bits of the unchewed food
> called cud and chews it completely
> this time before swallowing it again.
> The cud then goes to the third and
> fourth stomachs, the omasum and
> abomasum, where it is fully digested.
> Some of this digested food enters
> the bloodstream and travels to a bag
> called the udder, where it is made into
> milk that will come out of her teats,
> while the rest goes towards the cow's
> nourishment."[1]

Meditating on God's word nourishes and
strengthens us. It also nourishes and strengthens

others through our spiritual "teats." What an awesome God we serve! Let us marinate our bad ways in the Word of God!

Use the following scriptures to mediate on God's unfailing love.

Psalm 48:9 NIV: "Within your temple, O God, we meditate on your unfailing love."

John 3:16 KJV: "For God so loved the world that he gave his only begotten Son, that whosoever believeth in Him should not perish but have everlasting life."

1 John 3:1 NIV: "See what great love the Father has lavished on us that we should be called the children of God! And that is what we are!"

1 John 4:8 NIV: "Whoever does not love does not know God because God is love."

1 John 4:16 NIV: "And so we know and rely on the love God has for us. God is love. Whoever lives in love live in God, and God in them."

1 John 4:18 NIV: "There is no fear in love. But perfect love drives out fear, because fear has to do with punishment. The one who fears is not made perfect in love."

1 John 4:19 NIV: "We love because He first loved us."

Galatians 2:20 NIV: "I have been crucified with Christ and I no longer live, but Christ lives in me. The

---

life I now live in the body, I live by faith in the Son of God, who loved me and gave Himself for me."

Jeremiah 29:11 NIV: "For I know the plans I have you,' declares the Lord, 'plans to prosper you and not to harm you, plans to give you hope and a future."

Jeremiah 31:3 NIV: "The Lord appeared to us in the past saying, 'I have loved you with an everlasting love; I have drawn you with unfailing kindness."

John 15:13 NIV: "Greater love has no one than this: to lay down one's life for one's friend."

Psalm 86:15 NIV: "But you, Lord, are a compassionate and gracious God, slow to anger, abounding in love and faithfulness."

Psalm 136:26 NIV: "Give thanks to God of heaven. His love endures forever."

Romans 5:8 NIV: "But God demonstrates his own love for us in this: While we were still sinners, Christ died for us."

Use the following scriptures to mediate on God's works and mighty deeds:

Psalm 77:12 NIV: "I will meditate also of all thy work and talk of thy doings."

Psalm 111:1–3 NIV: "Praise the Lord! I will give thanks to the Lord with all my heart, In the company of the upright and in the assembly. Great are the works of the Lord; They are studied by all who delight in them. Splendid and majestic is His work, And His righteousness endures forever."

Revelation 15:3 NIV: "And they sang the song of God's servant Moses and of the Lamb: Great and wonderful are Your works, O Lord God Almighty! Just and true are Your ways, O King of the nations!"

CHAPTER 8
Praise and Worship

Praise is the act of expressing admiration, approval, and commendation unto God.

The songwriter William Murphy wrote the following words:

> "Praise is what I do when I want to be close to you. I lift my hands in praise. Praise is who I am. I will praise You while I can. I'll bless You at all times. I vow to praise You through the good and the bad. I'll praise you whether happy or sad. I'll praise you in all that I go through because praise is what I do cause I owe it all to you."

When you express adoration and approval to God, He draws near to you. God inhabits the praises of His people. In James 4:8 KJV, we read, "Draw nigh to God, and he will draw nigh to you. Cleanse your hands, ye sinners; and purify your hearts, ye double minded."

The story of Jehoshaphat in 2 Chronicles 20:1–29 will be our focal point here. We will read, study, pray, and glean life applications. The first and second books of Chronicles carry a central theme: obedience to God brings blessings, and disobedience brings disaster and defeat. Jehoshaphat was one of the righteous kings of Judah. He feared God, and he used the mighty weapon of praise to defeat Israel's enemies. Let us recap the story.

Jehoshaphat learned that his enemies had united forces to attack and destroy Israel. Fear gripped Jehoshaphat, and he sought the council of the Lord. Then he proclaimed a *fast* throughout all Judah. The people of Judah and Jerusalem gathered themselves together to seek the Lord's help. Then Jehoshaphat led the people in *prayer.* Jehoshaphat reminded God of His Word and His promise to the children of Israel, and he declared to the Lord, "We do not know what to do, but our eyes are on You." And the Lord answered speedily, saying that the battle was His and not theirs. He then gave the people specific instructions. After the

Lord spoke, the king and the people *worshipped* God. The Levites stood up and *praised* God with loud voices. Then they rose up early in the morning and went into the wilderness. Jehoshaphat gave the charge for war; he said, "Believe in the Lord your God so shall ye be established, believe His prophet so shall ye prosper." Then Jehoshaphat consulted with the people and selected singers unto the Lord. They praised the beauty of holiness as they sent singers out to the army to say, "O give thanks unto the Lord; for he is good: for his mercy endureth forever." (Psalm 136:1 KJV) And when they began to sing, the Lord set ambushes against the enemy of Israel, and they killed each other. When Israel entered the enemy camp, everyone was dead, and so they collected the spoils. There were so many spoils it took them three days to gather it all. The Bible says that God made them to rejoice over their enemies and gave Jehoshaphat peace in all the surrounding territory.

What principles from studying this story can we apply to our lives today to experience victory? Let us list a few.

- In all our ways, we must acknowledge God. He will direct our path. Jehoshaphat sought the Lord and called a fast.

- God is a Promise Keeper; Jehoshaphat prayed about the promises of God.
- God inhabits the praises of His people. Jehoshaphat defeated his enemies with praises unto God.
- God hears and answers prayers. The Lord answered Jehoshaphat prayer.
- God honors fasting done in accordance with His Word. A prophetic word and word of knowledge was given to Jehoshaphat and the people, and the word came to pass.

Once we study and identify the principles in the Word of God, we must take ownership of the principles through prayer. We put our name in it to make it personal. Say the following prayer points:

- Father, my enemies have come against me, my family, and my ministry. Just like Jehoshaphat, I am afraid, but my eyes are on You.
- Lord, show me what to do as I fast and pray and seek Your face.
- Lord, I believe you inhabit the praises of Your people as stated in Psalm 22:3.
- Father, I believe that my praise is a weapon, and it annihilate my enemies.

- I praise You, my Deliverer, my Fortress, and my Strength, the Lion of the tribe of Judah, the Word made flesh, the great I AM, the King of kings and the Lord of lords. You are the Lord of all, the Most High God, and the Prince of Peace. You will never leave me alone.
- You are my refuge, my rock, my defense, my salvation, and I trust You.
- You, Oh God, cause me to triumph over my enemies.
- Thank You for the spoils that my enemies bring into my life. I will use them to bring You glory and honor and praise! Amen!

A declaration is a written or oral indication of a fact, opinion, or belief. An affirmation is a declaration that something is true. It is a form of self-enforced mediation. As we meditate on the mighty acts of God, our minds are renewed, and we are transformed to prove that which is the good, acceptable, and perfect will of God for our lives.

The website The Spiritual Life defines *worship* as "an act of attributing reverent honor and homage to God" (https://slife.org/christian-worship/). In the New Testament, various words are used to refer to the term *worship*. One is *proskuneo* (to worship), which means to bow down to God or kings.

The Lord seeks those who worship Him in spirit and in truth. What does it mean to worship God in spirit and in truth? In spirit means that we are genuine with our adoration, reverence, and homage to the Lord. We know we are genuine when His attitude shows up in everything we do and becomes our lifestyle.

In truth means that our worship is based on the Word of God—caring for our family, helping others, forgiving offenses and unfair treatment. When we worship in truth, we have power to overcome life challenges and be an encouragement as a witness of God's faithfulness and love. When God is the priority in your life, His presence is tangible in all that you do. In His presence is fullness of joy. Your life is no longer ordinary because of the presence of God. In the throne room of God, His presence brings revelation as they cry "Holy, holy, holy!" for all eternity as they experience another facet of God.

"The four and twenty elders fall down before Him that sat on the throne, and worship Him that liveth forever and ever and ever, and cast their crowns before the throne, saying, Thou art worthy, O Lord, to receive honor and glory and power: for thou hast created all things, and for your pleasure they are and were created." (Revelation 4:10-11 KJV).

The effects of worship in our lives transforms us through the revelation power of the presence of God.

Our approach to God on a daily basis should be a replica of the tabernacle of Moses. There is a way to God or a pattern, and the tabernacle of Moses was the replica of the tabernacle in heaven. Now that the Blood of Jesus is on the mercy seat once and for all we can come boldly into the presence of God.

Flow of Worship

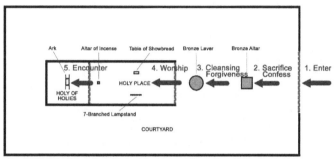

- Be sure to enter His gates with thanksgiving.
- Sacrifice and confess your sins. Repent daily by asking forgiveness; just like we bathe our physical bodies daily, we should bathe our spiritual bodies as well.
- Cleansing and forgiveness are represented by the bronze laver or basin. We receive His forgiveness and cleansing by faith with thankfulness.
- Worship is the next step. As the priests tended the lamps, the table, and the altar of

incense, we offer regular thanksgiving and praise to God in the Holy Place as a sweet fragrance before Him.

- Encounter with God in the Holy of Holies. This is where the transformation happens causing you to do it again and again. We were created to worship God.

CHAPTER 9

Fellowship with the Saints

As iron sharpens iron, like-minded people and accountability partners are what you should identify amongst saints. This interaction or fellowship is an important part of your Foundation Check, and here's why.

When your knives get dull, what do you do? You get a sharper knife and rub the two together until the dull one becomes sharp. It is the same with fellowship with other saints. It is very important to our spiritual growth to participate in small groups because we are better together. There is a gift, word, or smile that you have for me and I for you.

"Give, and it shall be given unto you; good measure, pressed down, and shaken together, and running over, shall men give into your bosom. For with the same measure that ye mete withal it shall be measured to you again." Luke 6:38 KJV

God blesses you using people, so if you do not respect and interact and be friendly, you will not have friends, and your blessings and spiritual maturity will be stunted.

Like-minded people are so powerful when it comes to productivity. For example, in the Bahamas, the Bay Street Boys dominated in real estate. Together they were able to buy prime property and experience great wealth by association. Another example is the disciples who cast their nets on the other side at Jesus's command, and they caught a great many fish; so much so that they called their associates to share in the catch. Like-minded people are the foundation of the creation of wealth and riches and experiencing productivity in one's life.

Fellowship of the saints will assist you in identifying like-minded people who love the Lord and have the same faith as you. Like-mindedness promotes the power of agreement. This principle unifies people, and they are able to accomplish anything they set their heart too.

We see this in the story of the Tower of Babel. The people were unified in their desire to build a tower up to heaven. Like-minded people are needed to be successful in your assignment for God. It is always by the people for the people.

Accountability partners are people who keep you focused on your dreams and goals. They keep you focused and on the right track based on the goals and dreams you have shared with them. They are the ones who hold you accountable for what you promise to do. Without a good accountability partner, you will find yourself not making much progress, especially if you are not self-motivated.

These elements must exist in your Foundation Check to give you a better chance of winning at life! Finding these qualities in a person is one thing but finding them in a believer like yourself is another level of productivity and favor.

The Bible encourages us to not forsake the assembling of ourselves together. In Hebrews 3:13 KJV we read, "But exhort one another daily, while it is called today; lest any of you be hardened through the deceitfulness of sin."

To exhort is to call to one's side, to summon or address, to speak to or admonish, to comfort, console, encourage, strengthen, teach, and instruct in the way of the Lord. So, in the fellowship of the saints, we get to sow good seeds in good ground so that when we need it, we have it. We get to pray one for another and with each other, and prayer changes things, people, and places.

Fellowship of the saints keeps you rooted and grounded in the things of God and gives us godly friends who strive to be like Christ. Check your foundation and ensure that fellowship with the saints exist in your life and does not lie dormant.

PART 3
Check for Cracks

In the Greek sin means missing the goal and scope of life.

A crack in your foundation indicates sin at its infancy stages. But if left alone, it will inevitably cause the structure to fall. The flesh is the gateway for sin. *Foundation Check* will assist you in identifying the sin that so easily besets you. You cannot continue to build a structure with sin in the foundation. Sin will begat sin.

Ann Ormley's hymn The Wise Man, and the Foolish Man offers these lines:
"The foolish man built his house upon the sand …
The rain came down and the floods came up,
And the house on the sand fell flat."

The rain is coming someday, and you must be able to weather the storms of life, or you will never complete your assignment. At the end of your life, your Creator may call you a "wicked and slothful servant." (Matthew 25:26 KJV) Yes, there can be servants who are wicked and slothful—not walking in their full potential. The church is full of them. You make it one less by changing your mind today! Once you have decided to change, let's move to the next step, which is acknowledgement!

To solve a problem, you first must acknowledge there is one. We are talking about cracks in your foundation that indicate sin. We have established that sin is missing the mark and goal of the life that God ordained for you. Galatians 5:19 says that the works of the flesh are these— Let me just stop right here and say where you put your energies manifests from secret to open shame and disgrace or open admiration and acclaim. Both require work; in other words, both require your involvement. Father God has given mankind dominion power. This is a power that rules. The Father of creation also gave us free will to choose where we place that power—in the devil's kingdom or back to the Father of light and life that gave it to us in the first instance.

Galatians 5:19 KJV "Now the works of the flesh are manifest which are these, adultery, fornication, uncleanness, lasciviousness, idolatry, witchcraft, hatred, variance, emulations, wrath, strife, seditions, heresies, envying, murders, drunkenness, reveling, and such like of the which, I told you before and I will tell you again, that they that do such things shall not inherit the kingdom of God."

No. Type	Meaning
WORKS OF THE FLESH	
1 Adultery	A married person having sex outside the marriage
2 Fornication	Unmarried persons having sex with each other
3 Uncleanness	Filthy, moral filth or lewd flashers, orgies
4 Lascioviousness	Acknowledges no restraints, readiness for all pleasure
5 Idolatry	Worship false gods, anything you spend more time with than GOD
6 Witchcraft	Spells, enchantments, rebellion of God's word, munipulation
7 Hatred	Seek to do bad to and for others
8 Variance	Strife, discord, contention
9 Emulations	A striving to equal or do more than others to obtain carnal favor.
10 Wrath	A strong feeling of hatred or resentment with a desire of vengeance
11 Strife	Bickering, discord, antagonism or quarreling
12 Seditions	A disagreement without love and intent to bring peace
13 Heresies	Any belief or practice that explicitly undermines the gospel
14 Envyings	A hostile feelings against someone because they have something
15 Murders	Termination of life
16 Drunkenness	Impairs judgment, lowers inhibitions and lead to regretable actions
17 Revellings	drinking parties late into the night that end with debauchery

Ann Ormley's hymn continues …

The foolish man built his house upon the sand,
The foolish man built his house upon the sand,
The foolish man built his house upon the sand,
And the rains came tumbling down.
The rains came down and the floods came up,
The rains came down and the floods came up,
The rains came down and the floods came up,
And the house on the sand fell flat.

CHAPTER 10
Sexual Immorality

Sexual immorality involves sexual sins. 1 Corinthians 6:18–19 KJV says, "Flee fornication. Every sin that a man doeth is without the body; but he that committeth fornication sinneth against his own body. What? know ye not that your body is the temple of the Holy Ghost, which is in you, which ye have of God, and ye are not your own?"

My body is for the Holy Ghost to control, that men may see my good works and glorify the Father, which art in heaven. Most sins offend people, but sexual sins offend your own body. They demonstrate that you do not love yourself and cannot truly love others because true self-love and self-care begin with knowing God.

These verses are addressed to believers—those who have accepted the Lord Jesus as their personal

Savior. When you do this, the Holy Spirit comes to live in your heart. When you have intercourse outside of marriage with a married or unmarried person, you have committed an act of harlotry. Harlotry is sexual sin done repeatedly as a way of life. Prostitution is a form of harlotry. This scripture is speaking to soul ties. Everyone that person has slept with, you are now sleeping with. That means there are numerous persons in your bed having sex with you. When the Bible speaks about two being one flesh, it is referring to the souls of those people becoming intertwined or joined. This is why couples who have been married for years begin to look and act like each other. They can sense when something is wrong; they know what their partner's actions mean without a word being spoken. Their souls are intertwined. They are emotionally connected and spiritually connected.

As born-again believers, our bodies are the temples of the Holy Ghost. What happens in temples? Prayer, worship, and sacrifice unto Almighty God. These actions are habits of a person that knows their body is a temple for God to dwell in. Don't live a lifestyle filled with sin and debauchery. If you do, you need a foundation check. Be mindful that Jesus is the solid rock on which we stand. All other ground is sinking sand.

Our lifestyles should be filled with prayer, worship,

and sacrifice unto God. People ought always to pray and not faint. Pray without ceasing. Pray the prayers of the righteous. People who do that get a lot done.

God is a Spirit. Those who worship Him must worship Him in spirit and in truth. Worship is an attitude and action of giving all honor and glory to God. You take no recognition or praise for yourself; you direct it all to God. Why? Because you know that it is His keeping power that keeps you alive and well.

To sacrifice is to go without for the sake of advancing the cause or agenda of God. Some examples of sacrifice might be to give up your right to food, sleep, or money so that people might know and experience God in their lives.

Sexual sins are one of the fastest ways to advance the kingdom of Satan. Demons cannot operate without a body or host. Therefore, when you have sex outside the commitment of marriage, Satan can use you to spread demonic influence over the earth. Children born out of such relationships have the same tendencies unless deliverance takes place.

Soul ties occur when two souls are netted together because of sex or deep emotional ties to one another. There can be good soul ties and evil soul ties. The purpose for soul ties, be they good or evil, is to advance an agenda. Unity and like-mindedness are powerful media in which to create success in any project. Your actions are your symptoms. Don't ignore or think lightly of your actions or the actions of your loved ones or people in your environment. Be vigilant and submit everything to God in prayer. Ask the Father, who knows the heart of every person, what course of action to take. The Bible puts it this way: "In all your ways acknowledge Him, And He will make your paths straight." (Proverbs 3:6 KJV)

CHAPTER 11
Idolatry

Idolatry is defined as what we spend most of our time doing other than spending quality time alone with God. There are several things we can worship other than God. I will mention a few. They are cell phones, our jobs, our children, our spouses and our ministries.

In today's fast-paced world of convenience and technology, we find that several gadgets can take up our time. One of the most common is cell phones. The young, the old, the rich, and the poor all have cell phones and spend hours aimlessly scrolling up and down the internet. This worldwide plague cuts into family time and makes people anti-social and lethargic. They have given control of their lives to cell phones.

Some of us live to work; our jobs and professions

consume our days and nights. Our careers and working hours are all we think about. Some people conclude that the more they work the more money they will have. Some work just for the love of it. Luke 16:13 KJV says, "No servant can serve two masters: for either he will hate the one and love the other; or else he will hold to the one and despise the other. Ye cannot serve God and mammon." Anything with two heads is a monster, and many of us have become monsters in our behavior because we are being torn between two lovers and feeling like a fool.

Prayer point: "Lord, I choose you."

We love our children, and we desire the best for them, but we cannot allow them to cause us to disobey the laws of God. Our adult children must take responsibility for their actions. We should not shelter them when they do wrong; rather, we must encourage them to do the right thing. We should always keep them in our prayers and hope that they will make the right choices with friends, in their business dealings, and in all areas of their lives.

A scripture to study on the topic of children is Proverbs 22:6 KJV. It's a very popular scripture and it reads; "Train up a child in the way he should go and when he is old, he will not depart from it." It means that, while your children are pliable and impressionable, teach them and demonstrate to them the ways of God. The lessons will stay with

71

them throughout their adult lives. In other words, bend the tree while it is young.

Prayer point: "Father let Your principles never leave my children."

We should never compromise the Word of God to save face with our children. We should allow God to train them even as adults.

Our husbands cannot come before God. There is a group of narcissist husbands who believe that their wives cannot hear God except through them. They deny their wives' individuality in God and see them as only instruments of their pleasure and every whim and fancy. The wives are seen as possessions and not people.

Wives, do not lose your identity in your marriage. Your calling and purpose will always be supported by God-fearing men. As a matter of fact, they will recognize it and ensure they nurture you to live your full potential in God. 2 Corinthians 6:14 KJV says "Be ye not unequally yoked together with unbelievers: for what fellowship hath righteousness with unrighteousness? and what communion hath light with darkness?"

Prayer point: "Father, I repent for my actions; make a way of escape so that I may walk in my full potential. Amen"

Husbands, do not be controlled by your wives. You are in charge and have the final say in every decision concerning the home and its affairs. Stand up in the power that God has given you to lead your family in the righteous paths of the Lord. Study this scripture: "But I would have you know, that the head of every man is Christ; and the head of the woman is the man; and the head of Christ is God." (1 Corinthians 11:3 KJV)

Prayer point: "Father, teach me how to lead my family with love."

The business of managing and shepherding God's people should never overstep the boundaries of your personal time with the Lord. Ministry is like a business; it takes time to grow and it is time consuming. But you must seek to be balance. Absolutely nothing can replace your personal time with the Lord. The bigger your ministry grows the more time you must spend with the Lord in prayer.

In Exodus 20:3 KJV we read, "Thou shall have no other gods before me."

Prayer point: "Father give me the grace to put you first in every choice I make."

CHAPTER 12

Unforgiveness

Unforgiveness is the holding of resentment for another person in your heart. Some people pass unforgiveness on from generation to generation.

Unforgiveness creates cracks in your foundation, and like the foolish person, those who do not forgive are building their houses on sand. They will not stand when the storm comes.

The Bible says, if your brother offends you, go to him quickly and work it out. Disappointments and disagreements are normal in all relationships. We are imperfect beings, and they will come to light in all relationships. The key is to forgive ahead of time before the offense comes. As a born-again believer, Holy Spirit will help you to forgive and forget. Forgiving entitles you to be forgiven for the offenses you exacted upon others. Forgiveness is a two-way street so to speak; you must give to receive. We are all in the flesh; therefore, we will all make mistakes.

Unforgiveness is a prison of pain and misery because of rehearse offenses in your mind. You hold to the rights of a victim as if it were a prize. This offense may have occurred years ago, but you did not let it go; now it hinders your progress in the things of God. Unforgiveness keeps you stagnant. Forgiveness is not for the other person; it is for you. It is your ticket to success!

Unforgiveness is a gateway for sickness and disease. Unresolved issues and pent-up anger leads to distrust and animosity toward even strangers who have done nothing wrong to you. Unforgiveness can leave you in a state of paranoia to the point that you shut out those who genuinely want to help. Unforgiveness is a prison of doubt, pain, and agony that will continue to fester until you release the offense, and the best way to do that is to follow the advice in Matthew 18:15–17 KJV. "Moreover, if thy brother shall trespass against thee, go and tell him about his fault between thee and him alone: if he shall hear thee, thou hast gained thy brother. But if he will not hear thee, then take with thee one or two more, that in the mouth of two or three witnesses every word may be established. And if he shall neglect to hear them, tell it unto the church: but if he neglect to hear the church, let him be unto thee as a heathen man and a publican."

We must give forgiveness to receive forgiveness. Study this scripture in Ephesians 4:32 KJV "And be ye kind one to another, tenderhearted, forgiving one another, even as God for Christ's sake hath forgiven you."

Prayer point: "Father give me a heart that forgives. Amen."

CHAPTER 13

Bloodline

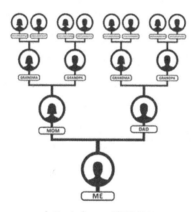

shutterstock.com · 1284786205

Proclivity to certain sins can be the result of unresolved issues in your bloodline. Here are some examples. My father's father never married my father's mother. My father had a child out of wedlock, married, then divorced. I, his daughter, had a child out of wedlock, married, and am now divorced.

My grandfather on my father's side died at seventy-eight, my father died at seventy-eight, my father's brother and sister, who had the same father, also died at seventy-eight.

These are not coincidences; these are bloodline issues. There is some evil covenant in the bloodline that must be broken. The sin of fornication and promiscuity ran rampant through my bloodline on my father's side and, in some cases, on my mother's side. And it showed up in me and my brothers.

Bloodline issues are very real and detrimental in many families. Incest, murder, witchcraft, these sins look for continuity in future generations. That's the goal of bloodline issues. The bloodline prayers I use are by Intercessor James Kawalya who contends in the courts of heaven and offers prayers on YouTube. Additional information can be found in the book "Courts of Heaven" by Robert Henderson.

This trouble in your bloodline may be the result of some relative who has died or who is still alive who has maintained a covenant with witches or warlocks promising sacrifice of children to continue their reign of terror. Black magic, sorcery, and all its other forms of evil are used to kill, steal persons' husband or wives, and manipulate and control persons for selfish gain, usually money or power.

Then there are word curses during which people speak over you and declare that you will be just like your "no-good father", or you will be a "whore like your mother". They say that "you will never amount to anything good."

Fraternities and lodges have evil pledges of alliance to evil altars, acts, and pledges that, if not cancelled, will show up in your life sooner or later.

CHAPTER 14
Childhood Trauma

Here's my story! It was a beautiful summer break on the beautiful island of Nassau in The Bahamas. I was on summer break from high school, and I had just landed a job for the summer at my favorite place, Scoops Ice Cream Parlor, which was owned by the McCartneys. I loved their menu of cakes, ice-cream, sandwiches and salads, especially turkey salad. Scoops was always my favorite place to visit on weekends so imagine my joy to get a job there for the summer. I got to eat all my favorite foods during summer break and get paid for it! I was in heaven!

Well, of course I had duties to perform in between eating. I felt as if I had won a million dollars. My world was vibrant and alive, and to top things off, I did not have to go to school for weeks. It could not get any better than that!

Then, suddenly, I glanced out of the shop window and noticed my mother looking bewildered as she sat outside in her car. I went out to see her. I said, "Mom, I did not know you were passing by for lunch." Her only response was, "Who am I and where am I?"

I was paralyzed. Shock and fear ran through my body as I tried to decipher what was going on with mom. My countenance went immediately from joy to great concern. What was happening with my mother? My mind could connect only to the extreme mental abuse she was experiencing because of an unfaithful husband. She experienced so many traumatic encounters with other woman. My world came crashing down as I tried to understand with the little wisdom and knowledge I had about the cause and how best to assist my mom at this moment. As suddenly as she had arrived, she drove away.

It was not until later in life that the symptoms of this encounter showed its ugly face as young men began to have an interest in me. I displayed a cold and nonchalant demeanor. I had absolutely no interest in marriage and very little in the opposite sex because of what I had seen my mother go through. I did not realize it at the time, but it became very evident the older I got. I was a tomboy and had low self-esteem. I did not trust anyone. *Marriage* was a bad word for me; I did not need it. From what I had seen, I believed men caused a lot of pain, and I was not going to let *anyone* hurt me.

So, I closed my heart and locked myself in the pain and the trauma. I buried it deep thinking it was dead forever, but it wasn't. It showed up in so many ways—disrespect, acting out, low self-esteem, lack of self-love, no self-realization, no purpose just to name a few. I was just existing, going through the motions aimlessly until I decided to make Jesus my Lord for real!

My father was not a predominant figure in my life so when I met my heavenly Father and started to develop a relationship with Him, I started to trust people again because I found my heavenly Father trustworthy. I experienced real love for the very first time through all the many relationships, heartache, and pain. My relationship with Father God surpassed them all.

I have never met anyone like God. He brings joy to my heart and peace to my soul. Father God started the process of healing my wounded soul so many, many years ago, and God has done a marvelous work in me. The rejection, rebellion, lust of the eyes, lust of the flesh, disrespect for authority, wanting my own way—it all faded and subsided as I worshipped Him and gave Him my heart to control. I have not arrived, but I must say that, at this junction and every junction of my life, God is the best and will always be the best thing that ever happened to me. I owe Him my life!

And so, you see, any form of trauma at any stage of your life is a gateway for destruction. It could be any adverse event that occurs during childhood. Examples might be neglect, abandonment, sexual abuse, emotional abuse, physical abuse, witnessing the abuse of a sibling or parent, or living with a parent who experiences mental health issues.

My childhood trauma was witnessing mental abuse toward my mom. This escalated to a point at which she did not know where she was or who she was. I can see it in my mind's eye right now as if it happened yesterday, and this happened over thirty years ago. I am just now categorizing it as childhood trauma. It leaves holes in your soul that only God can heal.

PART 4

Repair Check √

To move into a place of healing and restoration, we must investigate and apply the benefits of mind renewal, repentance, declarations, decrees, and affirmations. This includes applying and maintaining.

Before we get into that, let's prepare your statement of findings. Based on all that we have done, we must prepare this statement to ensure that we apply our efforts correctly and obtain optimum success.

As you prepare this statement, please, if you love yourself (want the best for yourself), be honest with yourself. To thine own self be true!

Complete the following form describing your mental state and needs in relation to each chapter. Email your responses to foundation√@gmail.com.

Chapter Title	Need help (√)
The Big Picture	
The Holy Ghost's Role	
The Growth Process	
Prayer	
Fasting and Prayer	
Personal Bible Study	
Meditation	
Praise and Worship	
Fellowship with the Saints	
Sexual Immorality	
Idolatry	
Unforgiveness	
Bloodline	
Childhood Trauma	

CHAPTER 15

Mind Renewal

"For as he thinketh in his heart, so is he: Eat and drink, saith he to thee; but his heart is not with thee." (Proverbs 23:7 KJV) Have you accepted Jesus Christ as your Lord and Savior? Have you confessed with your mouth and do you believe in your heart that Jesus Christ is Lord? Romans 10:9 KJV. If you believe that you have accepted Jesus as your Lord and Savior your behavior will demonstrate it. Let's investigate how, by studying the word *heart*.

A careful study of the Word of God will show you that, when the Bible speaks about heart, it is referring to the mind. This is the immaterial part of us that houses our thoughts, imagination, will, desires, memories, understanding, intellect, emotions, and reasoning abilities.

You are affected by what you allow through your

gates. These gates are the eyes, nose, mouth, ears, and skin. Proverbs 4:23 KJV says, "Keep thy heart with all diligence; for out of it are the issues of life."

Be intentional in what you allow through your gates because what you allow eventually comes out. Therefore, determine the results you want and choose only those thoughts that will take you there.

Maybe you have been a person who has used cuss words most of your life like Peter in the Bible. How do you stop? It starts with the mind; every action begins and starts with the mind. Did you grow up in an environment in which there was cursing all the time? This garbage, so to speak, was entering your ear gate for most of your childhood. You have been fed a steady diet of cuss words, so when you became a teenager, it became natural to do the same thing. If it is not stopped, this bad habit will carry on with your children and so on and so forth.

To break this evil cycle, you must interject a new thought. You need to replace your current thoughts with the Word of God. Life and death are in the power of our tongues, and we can use it to speak life or death to situations. You must decide daily, minute by minute, how you will use your tongue and most importantly what thoughts you will allow into your mind. The key is to identify where you want to go and speak life to what will take you there and speak death to what will not.

Personal Bible study is targeted toward personal issues. You can use the tools in the Quality Check section of this book to replace a bad thought with a God thought. The areas you have identified in the Check for Cracks section of this book, should be your Bible study topics. During Bible study you are getting to understand. This understanding infuses your prayer life which sets you free from all vices. You do not lose belly fat by targeting your legs. You must work on the problem area. If you have a tumor in your stomach, you do not seek an operation on your lungs. So, confront your issues with fire and force in your secret place.

To meditate is to mutter, speak, and ponder over the Word of God in your mind and utter the Word of God with your mouth. Your words have creative power. We were created like our Father God. He is a Creator, a King. He spoke everything into existence, and you have that same power.

You must practice pulling thoughts down. This means that no thought in your mind should be higher or more constant than the thoughts of Jesus Christ. In other words, there should always be thoughts of praise, adoration, admiration, and thanksgiving in your mind 24/7 unto Almighty God. The Bible says that those who experience perfect peace always have their minds focused on Christ. This means that, once your focus is Christ, nothing will be missing or broken in your life. Try it and tell me if it works. I guarantee it will! Money back guarantee! God can never and will never fail those who put their trust in Him.

You are worth it! Embrace this process and be the best you can be!

CHAPTER 16

Repentance

Repentance is a heartfelt conviction of sin, or contrition over the offense to God, a turning away from the sinful way of life and a turning to a God-honoring way of life. Daily repentance is paramount to optimizing your success. We sin all the time knowingly and unknowingly. We must be open to the leadership of Holy Spirit to expose all iniquity in our hearts. Once the Holy Spirit reveals it to you, He will empower you to overcome.

Godly grief leads to life, and worldly remorse leads to death. Worldly repentance is sorrow for being caught and no desire to change what caused the sin in the first place.

David wrote Psalm 51 because he was found guilty of adultery and premeditated murder. David asked the Father (in verse 10) to create in him a clean heart and renew the right spirit within him. This means to clean his thoughts, will, imagination, desires, memory, understanding, emotion, and reasoning ability. You see, David saw a beautiful woman bathing. It did not matter to him that she was another man's wife. Because he was king, he used his authority and called for the woman to have sex with him. So, his eye gate offended him. Through that gate entered lustful desire for another man's wife. The right spirit encompasses truth, respect, and humility, the wrong spirit David was battling was lust of the flesh, selfishness, and deceit. David asked the Lord to purge him with hyssop, which means to remove the sin from his heart. Sin started in his thoughts; therefore, his thoughts needed to change. This is how it works for us as well! Repentance and mind renewal go hand in hand. You cannot do one without the other.

CHAPTER 17
Declare and Decree

Job 22:28 KJV says, "Thou shalt also decree a thing, and it shall be established unto thee: and the light shall shine upon thy ways." This means that, if we pronounce something to be, God will make it so.

Declaring and decreeing are powerful tools in correcting wrongs by bringing you into alignment with the perfect will of God. But it first starts with a desire. That is why, in the previous chapter on repentance, I explained how David asked the Lord God Almighty to create in him a clean heart and renew the right spirit. Remember that the definition of *heart* is the mind, the place that houses our memories, understanding, thoughts, imagination, intellect, emotions, will, desire, and reason. David requested a clean or pure heart because the old one was getting him in trouble with God. David realized, through his life experiences, that God is the greatest power and life. He realized without Him, there is no life at all. So David ensured that, wherever he shut God out, he rectified the situation immediately. This is why God said that David was a man after His heart. In other words, David pursued having a heart like Father God's. David desired that his ways pleased the Father, and the only way to do that is to have the Father's thoughts, imagination, desires, will, emotions, ability, and intellect. What makes God mad must make us mad. We must see the world through the eyes of God. We must carry memories of when He delivered, healed, and set us free in the past knowing that He can and will do it every time you need Him. He does this because He is the Great I Am. David knew, through the many battles and triumphs, that, since God was for Him, no one could defeat him.

So here's how it works: With an audible voice and the authority of a son of God backed by the understanding that Bible study brings, you speak and establish God's will in a situation on the authority of God's Word. Then Father God will bring it to pass. The universe will respond to your voice!

CHAPTER 18

Affirmations

Affirmations are thoughts that we embrace as truth. According to the English American Dictionary, to affirm is "to state that something is true." When applied to spiritual life, affirmation is a statement of truth which one aspires to absorb into his life. Affirmations are dynamic and practical; they are not wishful thinking.

An example of an affirmation is, *I am healthy, wealthy, and wise. I am walking in the power and authority of God's Word.* Another one is *Abraham's blessings are mines.*

When you open your mouth and speak these truths with an audible voice consistently, you are breaking strongholds in your mind and are becoming a new creation in Christ Jesus. You are already positioned as a new creation, but your faith brings it into manifestation. Remember that faith without work is dead. What are the works here? Prayer, fasting, affirmation, declaring and decreeing, and much more. All these are works—exertion of energy in the things of God. This is what it means to work out your salvation with fear and trembling.

CHAPTER 19

Apply and Maintain

I remember going to Weight Watchers many, many years ago just as so many women do. I was overweight and wanted to slim down. My clothes were not fitting right, my self-esteem was low, and I was just miserable. Once I followed the plan and lost the desired amount of weight, I faced the final challenge—MAINTENANCE! Wow what a big word. At first, I thought to myself this would be a breeze; I soon found out that was not so! I ended up putting the weight back on, much to my surprise.

Habits are powerful tools that you must steer in the direction of your *purpose* if you are to experience optimum success and fulfillment. You must make a habit of evaluating your thought life to see what to keep and what to replace. Are procrastination and slothfulness habits that have been in your life for a long time? If the answer is yes, you must be patient with yourself but set a course, a resilient action plan to counterattack the habit you seek to replace.

For example – say you want to replace going to lunch every Monday with a woman or man who is not your wife or husband? Let the individual know, respectfully and lovingly, that you will no longer be available for lunch. Then replace that time by going to lunch with your spouse. This is an example of being intentional in your walk with the Lord.

As it is with the Weight Watchers program, you must maintain a certain diet. Your physical diet always shows on the outside. You can look at people's stomachs and know that they drink sodas or love desserts. Overindulgence shows up on the outside for all to see. No matter how many garments you put on, what's underneath still shows.

It works the same way spiritually. You must begin with the end in mind. For example, you have a rage that leads to sin, and you want to correct that rage. You must go to the Word of God and get the scripture on anger that leads to sin. Study the scriptures to ensure that you understand and that you are applying correctly. Then you must decree, declare, pray, replace and affirm until the problem is no more. In other words, you must starve your bad habit of your energy. Let it die!

PART 5

Conclusion

Ann Ormley's hymn "The Wise Man and the Foolish Man" concludes with the following lines:

> So build your life on the Lord Jesus Christ,
> So build your life on the Lord Jesus Christ,
> So build your life on the Lord Jesus Christ,
> And the blessings will come down.
> The blessings come down as your prayers go up,
> The blessings come down as your prayers go up,
> The blessings come down as your prayers go up,
> So build your life on the Lord.

In 2 Peter 1:2 KJV, we read that Apostle Peter prayed that grace and peace be multiplied to us through the knowledge of God, and of Jesus our Lord. God is still answering his prayer today as you make this prayer your prayer.

The areas in your life that are decaying require the knowledge of God and Jesus our Lord. This knowledge that Apostle Peter is speaking to is specified: God and Jesus.

Father God is the Alpha, the Source, the Beginning of all creation. He is protector and Provider, and He has not told Jesus everything; for example, when the end will be. This is why we must study as much as we can about the Father because He is different from the Son. We cannot lump them altogether. If your source is in anything else but Father God, it's in the wrong place, and death is imminent. If your ideas and your reason for getting up in the morning are not wrapped up in the Source, the start of everything, you need to consider a reconnection because God is the Sustainer, and His will and His way must be followed. If you choose another way, you are disconnected from the Sustainer of life!

Jesus our Lord is the Savior of the world. Jesus volunteered to execute the salvation plan so that humankind could return to an intimate relationship with Father God. It was through intimacy that we came forth into existence spiritually and physically; and it is true intimacy we *must* return to in order to give birth to the agenda of God in the earthly realm.

You experience true intimacy only when you have reached the conclusion that God and God alone cannot fail you. Through much trial and error, your faith will find a resting place in God *alone*! Keep living and you will learn for yourself, if you have not learned yet, that all other ground is sinking sand!

Jesus learned obedience through the things He suffered; we learn the same way. Once you have suffered a while, you will be able to see the light and the hope of glory, you will be ready to commit the rest of your days to God alone! You don't need anything to supplement or compliment Him. He is it—full stop! You will find that you are complete in God. Scriptures say that you will find God if you search for Him with *all* your heart. That is all your thoughts, imagination, desires, will, intellect, understanding, emotion, and memory. All your heart! You must examine your thoughts as you seek after God. You must remember the goodness of God. You must tell your will that you want God's will. You must pray for your understanding to be enlightened to the things of God. You must tell your desires that you desire what God desires for you. This is how you delight yourself in the Lord; then He gives you the desires of your heart. It's in God alone that we live, move, and have our very being. Absolutely nothing else!

In scripture, Apostle Peter continued to explain to us how we shall never fall. Let's look at 2 Peter

1:3–10 (KJV). Peter says that God's divine power—no strength of our own—has already given us *everything we need* for life and godliness. But here it is again—it happens through *knowledge*. Verse four talks about God's promises. God promised that heaven and earth will pass away before one 'jot or tittle' of His Word is removed. That means that it is impossible for God to lie. If God said it, that settles it! The young people would say 'it's a movie'!

Apostle Peter tells us that the corruption that is in the world came through lust. We don't need it if we trust in the promises of God. If you do not trust, the devil always provides an alternate lifestyle. You must tell the devil *no*! Why settle for less when God has given you His *best*?

Apostle Peter continued to explain how you can reach optimum success in life. You need the following ingredients:

1. Diligence
2. Faith
3. Character and virtue
4. Knowledge
5. Temperance and self-control
6. Patience
7. Godliness
8. Brotherly kindness
9. Charity

Let's define and apply. I would like to say we should make room in our lives for improvement. Seek an area in your life to which you can apply these life-changing and life sustaining principles. Let's begin.

Diligence describes consistent, faithful repetition of a task daily until it becomes a way of life. For example, reading your Bible every day at around 5:30 in the morning for thirty minutes. The length of time is not the focus; the development of godly habits is.

Faith is your belief system, what you believe to be true. Faith always shows up in your actions. Identify the action(s) in your life that lack faith in God. An example would be listening to secular music. How can a song with lyrics that promotes sex outside of marriage bring glory to God? Once you have identified conflicts between your actions and scripture, that's a good place to make a change.

The steps for change are: -

1. Decide that a habit is wrong, and if you continue to embrace it, it will bring destruction to your life.
2. Pray and ask the Holy Spirit to help you.
3. Search out the scripture that stands against that sin.

4. Study the scripture for approval and correct understanding.
5. Replace the bad habit with a good one.
6. Decide on your goal and make an action plan to convert from secular music to true gospel music.
7. Be patient with yourself but keep on pushing toward your goals.
8. Seek out an accountability partner.

Character or virtue equates to integrity in your relationships. Like Father God's promises do, your promises should mean something. Do not make promises you cannot keep. Keep the ones you make. Honesty is always telling the truth, being transparent and upfront, not being deceptive and conniving. Here is an example: There is a thief at work, and you know who it is, but you do not want to speak up because you want to protect the person. That's an example of your self-righteousness, not God's. We must always tell the truth, no matter the cost.

Knowledge is information or facts about a certain subject. The knowledge we are focused on in this context is Father God and Jesus our Savior. How much do we know about them? For the first three days of every month, the Lord instructed me to go on a fast for knowledge. Here is my assignment: on the first day of the month, I study Father God; on the second day, I study Jesus; and on the third day, I study the Holy Spirit.

We need to ensure that we have a plan in place to know God. In Philippians 3:10 KJV, Apostle Paul says, "That I may know him, and the power of his resurrection, and the fellowship of his sufferings, being made conformable unto his death;" We need to get to know God. In these last and evil days when deception is at an all-time high, we need to know God because, if it were possible, even the very elect might be deceived. That's how bad it is, and it will get worse.

Temperance is self-control. We are spirit beings who are living in bodies and possess souls. The flesh we live in is enmity against God. This means that the flesh opposes the ways of God. For example, when the spirit of God in you tells you to fast and get up and read your Bible, the first opposer is your flesh. The flesh wants to do the opposite—sleep and eat. So, the control comes in when the Spirit of God gives you an instruction, and you must beat your flesh into submission. You must speak to your flesh and let it know who is in charge because, if you give it an inch, it will take a mile.

Patience is the ability to continue following God's last instruction until the next one comes. It's not lagging or running in front of God but walking in step with the Holy Spirit. Patience strengthens your submission to God's will and way. Patience enables you to move at the right time, and when your movements are synchronized with God's, nothing can stop you, all hindrances and blockages are removed, annihilated!

Godliness is imitating God. Our lives reverence Him when we follow Him, handling and conducting ourselves the way He would.

Brotherly kindness is of paramount importance because God blesses you through the hands of fellow humans, and your ministry will always be to God and humankind. All people are the objects of God's love, and so they should be yours as well. We must speak no evil of anyone and seek to be a blessing to all. We must celebrate and promote each other.

Charity is generosity and helpfulness motivated by love. Through love, everything you do has the best interest of others as a motive. This type of love never fails. It is patient, kind, and long-suffering. It is not rude and does not seek its own way. A lover is a giver!

When we focus on these principles and not the latest gossip, we will find that we are building a fortress of success around our lives. Success is defined as completing the assignment God sent you to earth to do! I have summarized the concept in the following table. Be sure to memorize, study, and apply the "equation." Make it a point of prayer daily and watch God Almighty come through for you!

FAITH + VIRTUE + KNOWLEDGE + TEMPERANCE + PATIENCE + GODLINESS + BROTHERLY KINDNESS + CHARITY + DILIGENCE = NEVER FALL

Ecclesiastes 12:13 KJV says, "Let us hear the conclusion of the whole matter: Fear God and keep his commandments: for this is the whole duty of man."

Saved or unsaved, we have a duty to our Creator; that's automatic because we did not create ourselves. Please consider your ways seriously and take time to read your Creator's book, the Bible, and decide where you want to go when the breath leaves your body—and it will. After all the *noise* in the market when the dust settles, it will be just you and your Creator, and He will ask you to give an account for the deeds you have done while you were in the body. Consider what you will say now and start over again if you must, by giving Father God your heart—every part—so that you can make your calling and election sure. Mark 8:36 KJV tells us, "For what does it profit a man to gain the whole world and forfeit his soul?"

Please take your Foundation Check seriously and soar into all that Father God has ordained for your life!

Blessings!

ON GOD'S HOUSE BAHAMAS YOUTUBE CHANNEL

Ways to Give

Deborah J Knowles
Commonwealth Bank
Nassau Bahamas
Account # 1011022820
Transit/Branch # 21101
SWIFT CODE COMWBSNS

Every Week Day

Mondays	Prayer
Tuesdays	Purpose
Wednesdays	Kingdom of God
Thursdays	Evangelism
Fridays	Sex Education

Remember to like, share and subscribe @ God's House! ★★★★★

Printed in the United States
by Baker & Taylor Publisher Services